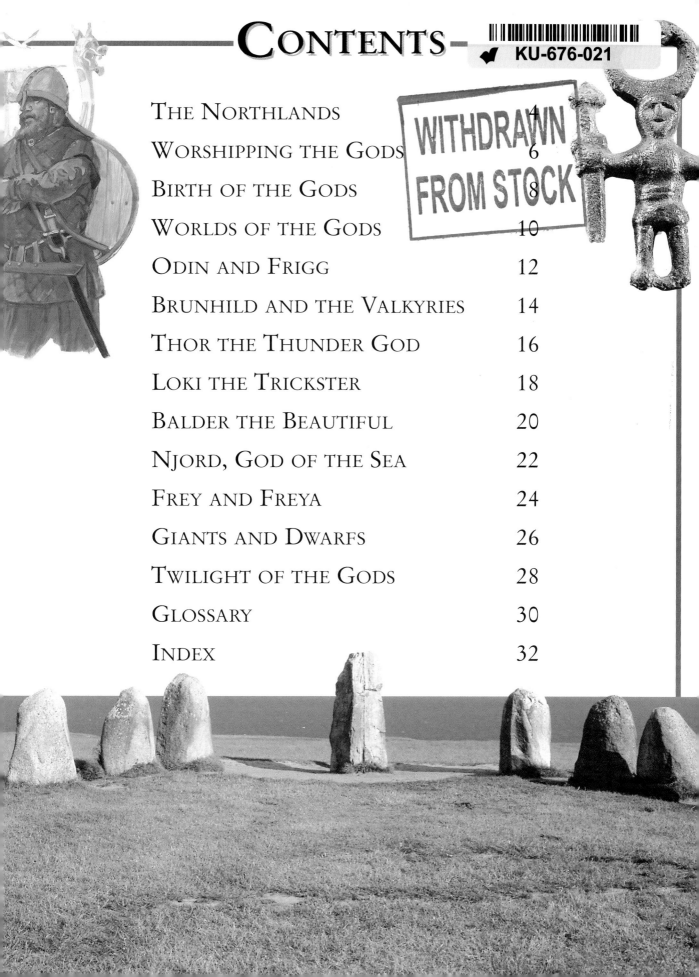

CONTENTS

THE NORTHLANDS 4

WORSHIPPING THE GODS 6

BIRTH OF THE GODS 8

WORLDS OF THE GODS 10

ODIN AND FRIGG 12

BRUNHILD AND THE VALKYRIES 14

THOR THE THUNDER GOD 16

LOKI THE TRICKSTER 18

BALDER THE BEAUTIFUL 20

NJORD, GOD OF THE SEA 22

FREY AND FREYA 24

GIANTS AND DWARFS 26

TWILIGHT OF THE GODS 28

GLOSSARY 30

INDEX 32

THE NORTHLANDS

T HE VIKINGS lived 1200 years ago in Scandinavia, in the lands that are now Norway, Sweden and Denmark. These lands were poor and over-populated, so the Vikings took to the sea. They became pirates and raided other countries. They also became traders and travelled far across Europe to buy and sell goods – and slaves. They even crossed the Atlantic Ocean to America. Together with the Saxons and other Germanic peoples of northern Europe – the Northlands – they are known as Northmen or Norsemen.

EXCITING STORIES

Wherever they went, the Norsemen took with them their gods, and stories about them. The stories tell of a wild and often violent world, full of magic, monsters and heroes. Two families of gods and goddesses – the Aesir and the Vanir – were at war but eventually made peace. Many stories are about the chief god, Odin, his wife, Frigg, and his many sons.

Other stories tell how the world was created and how in time it would be destroyed in a great battle, in which the gods would perish (see page 28).

Norse stories were told aloud and passed from generation to generation by word of mouth. The Vikings did not write much, so archaeologists have had to find out about them from other remains, from their neighbours and from writers who lived in the lands they visited. These writers were mostly Christian. In time the Vikings gave up their old gods and became Christians, too.

WRITTEN IN RUNES

The Vikings and Saxons wrote in runes, an alphabet of letters that consist almost entirely of straight lines. The word rune means secret. Probably runes were first used by priests to write spells in magic rituals. Most runes were carved in wood but some were in stone (left) and many of these have survived.

POEMS, SONGS AND STORIES

Many Norse stories, or sagas, were recounted in the songs of bards or written down by Christian storytellers in collections of poetry, like those of the Icelander Snorri Sturluson (1179-1241). Characters from Norse legend, such as giants and elves, also survive in fairy tales. The composer Richard Wagner based a series of operas, called *The Ring of the Nibelungs*, on the exploits of the Norse gods, and the hero Siegfried (Sigurd), seen here fighting a dragon.

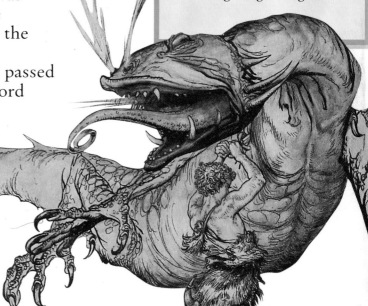

FAMILIES OF THE  VIKING GODS

YMIR
ice giant whose body formed the world

AESIR FAMILY

VANIR FAMILY

BOR
son of Buri, ancestor of the first gods

NJORD
god of the sea

LOKI
trickster and companion of the gods

ODIN = FRIGG
ruler and wisest of gods *goddess of women and mothers, wife of Odin*

FREY
god of fertility, brother of Freya

FREYA
goddess of fertility, sister of Frey

BRUNHILD
Valkyrie who was saved by Sigurd

HEL
ruler of the dead

THOR
thunder god of the sky

HEIMDALL
guardian of the rainbow bridge

TYR
god who bound the wolf, Fenrir

BALDER
beautiful god of light who was doomed to die

HODER
blind god of night who was tricked into killing Balder

HERMOD
brave god who went to Hel for his brother

▲ Two families of gods feature in Viking myths, the Aesir (sky gods) and the Vanir (earth gods). The myths also tell of Loki, who was Odin's friend, of warrior maidens like Brunhild, and of many other gods and monsters.

= MARRIAGE

5

WORSHIPPING THE GODS

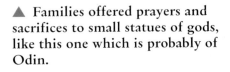

WE KNOW many stories about Viking gods and goddesses but little about how the people worshipped them. Viking religion varied from place to place, and there were probably few priests or religious leaders.

TEMPLES AND FESTIVALS

The ancient Egyptians, Greeks and Romans built stone temples and statues but the Northern peoples built mostly in wood, and wood does not last as long as stone.

No Viking temples have survived, though one at Uppsala, in Sweden, was described by a German historian called Adam of Bremen who lived more than a thousand years ago. He described a great festival that was held at the temple every nine years. Other temples must have rotted away when the old beliefs were abandoned or have been deliberately destroyed by Christian rulers who wanted to stamp out pagan worship.

HUMAN SACRIFICE

Some evidence of pagan rites has been found, including magic wells into which captives were flung. Close to the temple at Uppsala was a sacred grove where humans and animals were hanged in ritual sacrifices. Probably feasts, assemblies and sacrifices took place at the foot of giant trees, particularly ash trees.

▲ Families offered prayers and sacrifices to small statues of gods, like this one which is probably of Odin.

▼ The stones in this Viking burial site are arranged in the shape of a ship.

TREES OF LIFE AND DEATH

Trees were important in the Northlands. Timber was the most useful raw material for building homes and ships. But trees also had a magical significance. The people worshipped 'magic' trees, and hung sacrifices from the branches of trees in sacred groves. Christian priests later cut down these ritual trees.

▲ This pendant of a man holding a sword and two spears is probably a priest dedicated to Odin.

▼ A 7th-century Viking helmet, found in a grave ship. Helmets were usually made of leather and had no horns.

BURIALS AND BURNINGS

When a Viking died, some of his goods were placed in his grave and buried with him. These he would need in the afterlife. An early Norse custom was for a chief killed in battle to be burned in his own ship. Other warrior heroes were buried on ships inside earth mounds. On the battlefield, smoke from funeral pyres 'rolled up to the clouds'. Everything burned on the funeral pyre passed with the owner to Valhalla (see page 15). Some sacrifices included slaves, wives and horses.

7

BIRTH OF THE GODS

LONG BEFORE the first gods and humans appeared, the first being emerged, and from him came the world. In the beginning there was a land of ice, Niflheim, and a land of fire, Muspell. Where the two met, the ice melted and formed a giant called Ymir. From Ymir's arm came the first man and woman. From his legs came the frost giants. Ymir lived on milk from a cow, which also appeared from the ice. As the cow licked the ice, it melted, freeing a being called Buri. His son Bor was father of the first gods, Odin, Vili and Ve. The three gods then killed Ymir and used his body to make the world.

NIGHT AND DAY

Sparks thrown up from the land of fire formed the sun, moon and stars. Then the gods made time. Night – a giant's daughter – and her son, Day, were sent around the world in horse-drawn chariots. A girl and boy – Sun and Moon – also drove across the sky, chased by the great wolves Skoll and Hati. The Vikings believed that the world would come to an end when the wolves finally caught and swallowed the sun and the moon. Then the stars would die and all things end. This metal mould, used for making decorations on Viking

▼ Odin confronts Ymir. He and his brothers killed the ice giant, who represented the icy cold which the Norse people had to fight every winter.

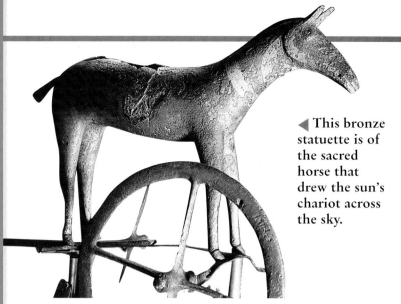

This bronze statuette is of the sacred horse that drew the sun's chariot across the sky.

helmets, shows the wolves swallowing the sky – which is represented by a warrior.

Odin is shown on this tapestry with an axe, the weapon of Viking warriors.

The giant's icy blood made the rivers and seas. His flesh formed the earth and his bones the mountains. His teeth and jaws turned to rocks and stones. Ymir's skull formed the sky, held up by four dwarfs (North, South, East and West). The gods created dwarfs from maggots in Ymir's dead body, and inside the earth's rocks the dwarfs lived ever after.

LAND OF THE VIKINGS

The mountainous lands of northern Europe have a savage climate. Winters are icy cold and there is almost no daylight for weeks on end. Wild storms batter the coasts. In the time of the Vikings, great forests covered nearly all the land. In them lived wolves and bears – and who knows what other monsters and mysteries? The Vikings admired strong gods and heroes who could fight the forces of nature, the giants and monsters of their imaginations.

WORLDS OF THE GODS

THE VIKINGS believed that the world was a flat disc surrounded by sea. Holding it in place was a giant ash tree called Yggdrasil, or the World Tree. Its huge branches spread above the heavens while its roots reached into the lands of the gods, the giants and the dead.

ASGARD, MIDGARD AND NIFLHEIM

Humans lived in Midgard, or Middle Earth. So too did the giants, elves, and the dwarfs, in their gloomy holes and caves. Above all of these lived the gods and goddesses, in glittering halls and palaces within their stronghold of Asgard.

▶ On the top branch of Yggdrasil, sat an eagle and coiled around its root was the huge serpent-dragon, Nidhogg. A squirrel named Ratatosk scurried up and down the tree, stirring up trouble between the eagle and its serpent enemy. Other creatures attacked Yggdrasil. Snakes gnawed its roots, goats and deer nibbled its leaves.

◀ This Norwegian wood carving shows a deer browsing on the World Tree.

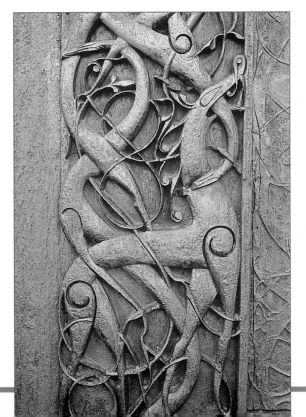

ELVES, SPRITES AND SPIRITS

The Vikings believed the natural world was full of elves, spirits and demons. Dark elves lived in caves and holes, and came out to do mischief. Light elves were helpful and good. Water sprites, called nixes, lived in rivers and streams.

House spirits, called kobolds, chopped wood, fetched water, fed cattle and brought good luck while no one was looking. People wanted the elves on their side, so they poured offerings of milk for them into little cup-shaped hollows on rocks or stone tombs.

Below, on the lowest of the world's three levels, was Niflheim, land of the dead. Around Midgard and Asgard swirled a huge ocean in which lurked the terrible World Serpent called Jormungand.

Between Midgard and Asgard stretched a shimmering rainbow bridge called Bifrost, which was guarded against attack from the giants of Midgard by the god Heimdall. He was a superb lookout. He could see for huge distances and hear the slightest sound – even grass growing, or wool on sheep. His horn blast aroused all worlds.

▼ The god Heimdall guarded the rainbow bridge to the heavens. His horn could be heard through all the worlds.

THE WORLD UNDERGROUND

Yggdrasil had three main roots. One grew down to a sacred spring in the land of the frost giants. This fountain of wisdom was guarded by the friendly giant Mimir. Odin drank its waters, but at the cost of one of his eyes.

A second root lay by another spring, the well of Urd. Three goddesses called Norns (right) lived by the well, continuously spinning the thread of fate. When one of their threads broke, a person died.

The third root led to Niflheim, the realm of the dead. This place of eternal dark, ice and snow was ruled by the goddess Hel and guarded by a dreadful bloodstained dog called Garm.

ODIN AND FRIGG

ODIN WAS the chief god and ruler of Asgard. He was god of wisdom, magic and poetry. Above all, he was lord of battles, the god of kings and warriors. Odin caused war on earth by throwing down his spear. He also chose the victor, and so warriors tried hard to please him. His followers, the Valkyries (see page 14), chose who died and went to Valhalla, a hall in Asgard reserved for those who gave their lives in battle.

THE WANDERER

Odin sat on a throne from which he could see all worlds at once. He travelled far and wide about the earth, but also heard news from two ravens who flew about the world and whispered its secrets to him. They were called Hugin (Thought) and Mugin (Memory). Odin often went in disguise, wearing a cloak and a big hat that shaded his face. He could even change his shape and visit the underworld. The Vikings believed that Odin would

A FIGHTING LIFE

Fighting and feuds were common among the Norsemen. There was not much good land to farm and settle, so many fought for land, for wealth, and for wives. Once won, their farms, homes, belongings

▼ Odin and his warriors rode through the sky bringing death to his enemies.

▶ This carved gravestone shows Odin riding the eight-legged Sleipnir.

▶ Odin was armed with a magic spear and an arm-ring. He was also known as Woden and Wotan. Wednesday is 'Woden's day'.

and families had to be defended. All Norsemen learned to fight. As warriors they gave loyalty in battle in return for their leader's help and protection. The best leaders won their battles and shared out the plunder.

lead the fight to save the world but that he would be defeated and eaten by the wolf Fenrir (see page 28).

GODDESS OF LOVE AND THE HOME

Odin's wife was the beautiful Frigg. Like her husband, she knew magic and could tell the future, but she was also a mother goddess who cared especially for women and children. Frigg was clever enough to make Odin do what she wanted. She was loyal, too, even though Odin had love affairs with other goddesses and humans. Frigg's name is remembered in Friday, a day that Germanic peoples thought was lucky, especially for getting married.

▶ A small statue of Odin. Notice his blind right eye, which he gave up in exchange for knowledge.

FENRIR, THE WOLF

It was predicted by the Norns that Odin would be killed by the great wolf Fenrir, so the gods tried to keep the beast chained. But it always broke free. To trick the wolf, they ordered an unbreakable chain from the dwarfs (see page 26). When finished, it looked like silk ribbon. The wolf was suspicious when the gods asked to tie him up to test the ribbon's strength. He agreed only if the god Tyr put a hand in his mouth while the deed was done. When he found himself securely bound, Fenrir bit off Tyr's hand.

BRUNHILD AND THE VALKYRIES

ODIN was attended by a band of warrior maidens, including the most beautiful, Brunhild. Armed with helmets, shields and spears, these Valkyries rode to battle on flying horses. On Odin's instructions, they directed the fighting, guarding warriors or letting them fall. Heroes who gave their life to the war god on the battlefield gained a place in Valhalla.

SLEEPING BEAUTY

During peacetime some of the Valkyries changed into gentle swans. One day Brunhild took off her feathers to swim in a forest pool. A king who was passing stole her feathers and agreed to return them only if Brunhild helped him to win a battle – against Odin's wishes.

Odin was furious. To punish Brunhild, the god pricked her with a magic thorn to put her to sleep in a castle ringed by fire. Although the brave Sigurd rode through the flames and saved her, Brunhild was no longer a Valkyrie, but an ordinary mortal.

▼ In this wood carving, Sigurd is roasting a dragon's heart. When he tastes the dragon's blood he finds he can understand birdsong – and in this way learns of the treachery of his companion – the dwarf Regin.

▲ Vikings imagined the Valkyries galloping through the wild Norse skies on horses whose manes dripped with dew or hail.

GOING BERSERK

Some Viking warriors lived together in fortresses that no woman could enter, and defended each other as brothers in battle. The berserks were special warriors, clothed in bearskins, who believed that Odin would save them from harm. Before a battle, they worked themselves up into a frenzy in which they felt no fear or pain. Berserk means bearskin. We still use the expression 'to go berserk' when anyone loses control of their temper.

▼ This Icelandic illustration shows Valhalla. You can see Odin in the doorway and animals in Yggdrasil's branches at the top.

VALHALLA

Fallen warriors spent the afterlife in feasting and fighting. Valhalla's golden walls were roofed with shields, held up by huge spears gleaming so brightly that they lit up the whole hall. The heroes sat at long tables, dining on meat and mead served by Valkyries. Each day the warriors rode out to battle and returned, healed of their wounds, for the daily feast. There were over 500 doors to Valhalla, wide enough for 800 men to pass through side by side.

▶ Brunhild welcomes a valiant hero into Valhalla, where he will live forever feasting with his fallen comrades.

▼ This silver-gilt pendant was worn on a chain. It shows a Valkyrie offering a drinking horn of mead.

THOR THE THUNDER GOD

THE VIKINGS loved and respected Thor. He was big, brave and immensely strong. He fought the monsters and giants who threatened the world, including the evil World Serpent, Jormungand.

GOD OF STORMS

Thor was Odin's oldest son. He was a sky god, who ruled the heavens. In his gloved fist, he carried a hammer which always hit its target and returned to his hand. Thor's hammer caused thunder and lightning. It could split rocks, and kill humans and giants. As the god rode across the heavens in a chariot pulled by goats, thunder rumbled.

◀ This little bronze statue is of Thor. Thor was a sky god, like the Roman Jupiter or Jove. Jove's day in the Roman week became our Thursday (Thor's day).

GIANT SLAYER

The serpent Jormungand, lying coiled around the world under the ocean, caused terrible storms and shipwrecks. Fighting trolls and giants was easy, but the serpent was a challenge to Thor. Once, when fishing in disguise with a giant called Hymir, Thor used an ox-head as bait to drag up the serpent from the ocean deeps. But the giant grew scared and cut the fishing line. So the serpent lived to fight again.

THOR THE VIKING

Red-bearded Thor lived like a Viking warrior. He fought hard and feasted well. He could eat an ox or two at a meal and once tried to drink the sea dry. As the sea shrank, it caused the first tides.

PROTECTOR OF HOME AND FAMILY

Thor stood for order and safety. His symbol was the oak tree and at Yuletide, the

Viking sailors respected Thor. They asked him to send fair weather with good winds and guide them over the ocean. When Vikings took new land to farm, they blessed it in Thor's name before building a home and sowing crops. Thor's wife, Sif, was a goddess of plenty and fruitfulness with hair like golden corn.

▲ Vikings wore little hammer charms for good luck, and with them blessed babies, brides and the dead. Brides wore red, which was Thor's favourite colour.

▶ When lightning flashed, the Vikings knew that Thor had thrown his hammer.

god's main festival, people burnt a great oak log to drive away the cold and dark of winter. As Thor defended Asgard, so he protected Norse farms and homes.

LOKI THE TRICKSTER

L OKI LIVED in Asgard, even though he was not a god but the son of fire giants. A great joker and entertainer, he was sworn blood brother of Odin. The gods often did what the cunning Loki suggested, sometimes with disastrous results. Eventually they learned that he was not just mischievous, but also untrustworthy. As they grew wary of him, so Loki became bitter, especially when they punished him for causing the death of the god Balder (see page 20). The gods chained him up, but he broke free. In the end, he caused the downfall of the gods, and led the giants against them.

FATHER OF MONSTERS

Loki's children were monsters. Among them were the serpent Jormungand, the wolf Fenrir and Hel, the goddess of death. Sleipnir, Odin's eight-legged horse, was another of his offspring. Like Odin, Loki could change shape. He appeared as a hawk, a seal, a fly, a horse, or an old woman.

SACRED HORSES

Norse people admired the speed and power of horses the fastest land animals they knew. Scandinavian people rode small, tough ponies over tussocky grass rocks and mountains. Their horses gave the

▼ This stone was part of a Viking forge. It shows Loki with his lips sewn up. He tried to cheat the dwarfs and this was how they punished him.

REBUILDING ASGARD

One day a rider came by and offered to rebuild the wall around Asgard, which had been destroyed in a war with the Vanir. In return he wanted the sun, the moon and the goddess Freya. The gods were horrified. But crafty Loki told them how they could get the work done without paying. They agreed the builder's terms, on condition that the work was finished on time. The builder said he would agree to the terms, provided his horse could help. This horse, Svadilfari, moved huge stones so easily that it seemed the builder would earn his reward. So Loki changed into a beautiful mare, lured Svadilfari away from the wall, and stopped the building work.

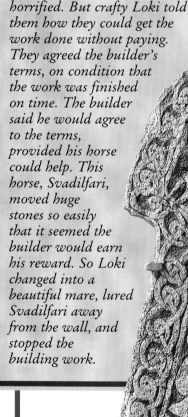

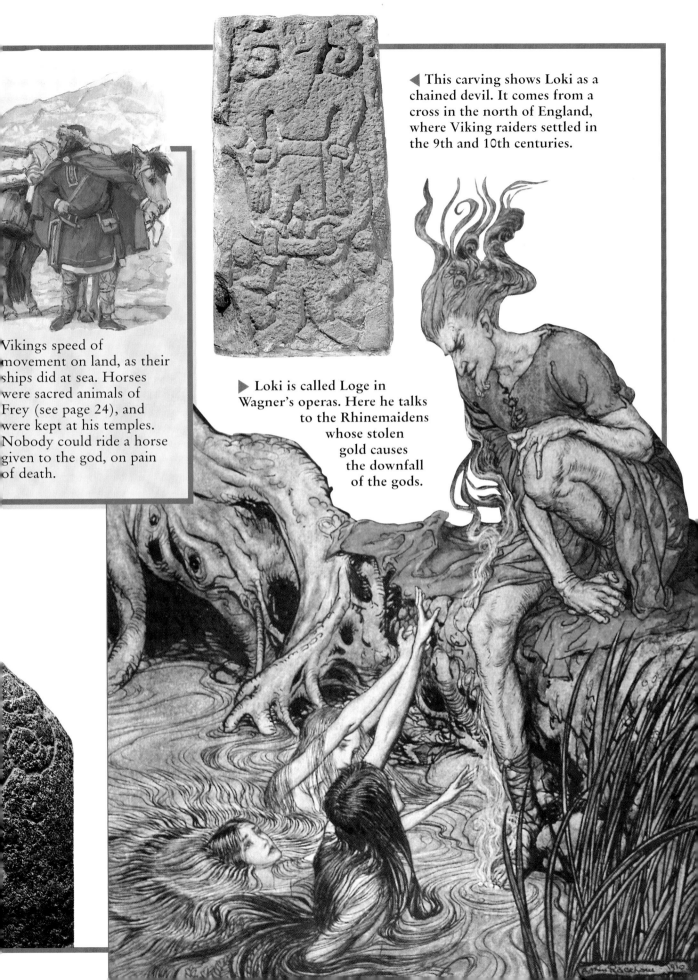

◀ This carving shows Loki as a chained devil. It comes from a cross in the north of England, where Viking raiders settled in the 9th and 10th centuries.

Vikings speed of movement on land, as their ships did at sea. Horses were sacred animals of Frey (see page 24), and were kept at his temples. Nobody could ride a horse given to the god, on pain of death.

▶ Loki is called Loge in Wagner's operas. Here he talks to the Rhinemaidens whose stolen gold causes the downfall of the gods.

BALDER THE BEAUTIFUL

BALDER, SON of Odin and Frigg, was god of light and twin brother to Hoder, the blind god of darkness. Kind, wise and gentle, Balder was the most handsome of the gods. Everybody loved him for spreading happiness and harmony. But Balder was troubled by bad dreams. Odin rode to Hel's hall to find out why, and was told that Balder must soon die. To save her son, Frigg asked everyone and every thing in the world to swear it would do him no harm. Believing Balder safe, the gods began throwing missiles at him, just to watch them avoid the target. But Loki, who was jealous of Balder, did not join in the fun.

LOKI'S TREACHERY

Loki transformed himself into an old woman and found out from Frigg that the mistletoe plant alone had not sworn to keep Balder safe. By magic, Loki made a pointed shaft from the plant and gave it to the blind god Hoder, to join in the gods' throwing game. With Loki guiding his aim, Hoder threw the shaft at Balder and the god fell dead.

Hermod, Balder's brother, went to the underworld to persuade Hel to let Balder go. If everything wept for him, said the goddess, he could return to life. Heralds went out from Asgard to ask all things – plants, animals, stones, metals – to weep for the beloved Balder. They did, all but one. A giantess in a cave, held to be Loki in disguise, refused and so Balder remained in the land of the dead.

▲ In this illustration of the legend, Balder is killed by a falling mistletoe bough.

► The horseman on this silver charm from Sweden may be Hermod, riding to Hel to plead for his brother.

◄ Here Loki guides the weapon held by Hoder as he pierces Balder's body with a spear of mistletoe.

MIDSUMMER FESTIVAL

Norse people held an important festival on midsummer's eve, the longest day of the year and the anniversary of Balder's death. Families built great bonfires and gathered outdoors to eat, talk and dance. Then they watched the sun set briefly, before it rose again. The story of Balder, god of light, recalls the daily setting of the sun, driven away by darkness. It was also a reminder of the short northern summer, before the arrival of cold, dark winter. In spring, winter's icy grip melts and everything drips with the thaw, just as everything on earth shed tears for Balder.

▶ Hermod borrowed Odin's magical horse for his journey to Hel's land of the dead.

NJORD, GOD OF THE SEA

THE VIKINGS were brave seafarers, but lived in fear of the serpent of Midgard who might stir up a violent storm at any moment. They knew the power of the sea, and its riches. Help from the gods was vital to them. Njord, god of the sea, belonged to the Vanir family. The Vanir gods were gentler than the Aesir. They looked after the fruitfulness of the earth and its people.

Njord watched over the coasts and gave the fishermen their catch. He controlled the winds, the waves and every ship that put to sea. People asked him to bless their boats and send plenty of fish to the coast.

AEGIR AND HIS DAUGHTERS

Beneath the sea lived the giant Aegir in a fine palace that glowed with treasure from sunken ships. Among his plunder was a magic cauldron, in which he brewed a mixture of beer and mead. Odin, Thor and the other gods loved to visit Aegir to share a drink and tell stories, before falling asleep from the effects of the heady drink.

Aegir was married to the goddess Ran and they had nine daughters. The Vikings thought there were nine different types of wave, and that each was produced by one of Ran's daughters. The daughters sang and danced to lure sailors to their underwater home.

FISHING

Most Norse peoples lived close to water – the sea or inlets of the sea such as fiords, lakes and rivers. Children learned to row and sail boats, and men became expert sailors, setting out along the coast

▼ While Odin's warlike family ruled the skies, Njord and the Vanir family were gods of the earth and seas. For Viking voyagers, and for fishermen, knowledge of the sea and the protection of its gods was vital.

WHOSE FEET?

Njord married a giantess called Skadi. Her father had been killed by the gods and she wanted to avenge his death. Rather than start another fight, the gods offered to let her marry one of them. She could choose whichever god she liked, but could see only their feet. Skadi chose the feet that she thought belonged to the beautiful young Balder. But, alas, she was wrong and wound up wedded to Njord, who was old and ugly – apart from his feet. Skadi, from the mountains, and Njord, from the sea, could not live long in each other's homeland. In the end they parted.

to visit market towns to sell their surplus farm produce. They also went fishing. Fish and seal meat were often smoked or salted to preserve them as a winter food supply, when fresh food was scarce.

▼ Viking longships were sturdy vessels with sails and oars. Important chiefs were sometimes buried in their ships, together with property they might want in the next world. This is the Oseberg ship which was found buried in Norway.

◄ This fearsome dragon head was found in Norway on a burial ship. Njord is said to have lived on a ship. He was a summer god, while his wife Skadi was goddess of winter.

FREY AND FREYA

MONG THE Norse peoples' favourite gods were the twins Frey and Freya, children of the sea god Njord. They could grant rich harvests and healthy cattle. Farmers asked Frey and Freya to bring them rain to water the growing crops and for sunshine to ripen them.

ALL THINGS GOOD

Freya was goddess of love and beauty, crops of grain and catches of fish. She saw that healthy animals and babies were born, and could foretell a baby's future, for she knew strong magic.

Frey granted peace and plenty. To make sure of good crops, people carried his image around their lands in a wagon. Nobody could carry weapons or shed blood on land dedicated to Frey, and no outlaw was allowed in his holy places.

FREY'S MAGIC

Frey's chariot was pulled by a magic boar made by the dwarfs. Its golden coat shone in the dark and lit up the sky as it flew over the earth. Frey also had a magic sword that moved by itself, a magic horse that could see in the dark and gallop through fire, and a magic ship that could carry all the gods and sail wherever it wanted. When not needed, the ship was folded up in a pouch.

▶ Freya liked gold. She had golden apples, a gold necklace that she bribed the dwarfs to give her, and she even wept golden tears when she was unhappy.

FREYA'S MAGIC

battlefields in it, choosing half of the dead warriors to join her in her hall in Asgard. The rest went with Odin to Valhalla. Freya had become a goddess of death as punishment for the way she bribed the dwarfs to give her a fabulous necklace they had made. She liked beautiful things and was also goddess of wealth. When sad, she shed tears of gold. Freya had a cloak of magic falcon feathers with which she could fly through all the worlds. This pendant shows Freya with her golden necklace, Brisingamen, around her neck. Its importance is stressed by its size.

Freya's chariot was pulled by two cats. She flew over

▲ This metal mould, used to produce a helmet decoration, shows two warriors. On top of their helmets are Frey's symbol, the wild boar.

▼ This tapestry shows Frey, wearing his royal crown. In his hand he carries an ear of corn.

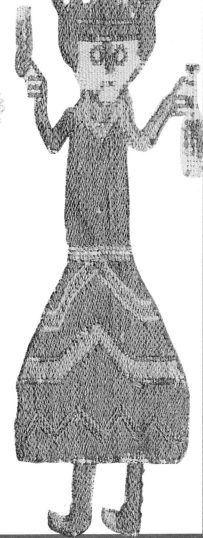

FARMERS

Norse farmers grew oats, barley and rye in lands too cold for wheat. They grew vegetables such as onions, cabbages and beans, and kept cattle, sheep, goats, pigs and hens. Women spent much of their day baking bread and cooking meat, fish and vegetables for the main meal, which was usually eaten in the evening, after the day's work was over.

GIANTS AND DWARFS

F ROST, FIRE and mountain giants came from the stronghold of Utgard. All the giants (and the trolls who were like them) were huge and as strong as the gods. They were like the forces of nature itself. People of the Northlands knew a landscape of mountains, caverns, glaciers, chasms and fiery volcanoes. Snow and frost smothered vegetation in winter, leaving bare ice and rock. This hostile climate and landscape threatened humans just as the giants menaced gods and people in the Norse tales.

THE CURSED RING

The dwarf Andvari forged a magic ring but Loki tricked him into giving it up, along with a huge hoard of gold. The dwarf cursed the ring which brought bad luck to anyone who possessed it. The hoard came into the hands of Fafnir, who had killed his father to gain it, and turned himself into a dragon to guard it. Sigurd, the son of the dead warrior, Sigmund, was brought up by a cunning smith called Regin, the brother of Fafnir. He forged a magic sword for Sigurd and encouraged him to kill the dragon. This he did, and later went on to rescue Brunhild.

◀ **This wood carving shows Sigurd the Dragonslayer killing Fafnir.**

MINING AND METALWORKING

The Vikings loved metals. An iron farm tool was almost as valuable as an iron sword. The craftsman who worked iron into shape in his fiery forge was the smith, and smiths were both respected and admired for their seemingly magical skill. Gold and silver were even more highly prized. Wealthy warriors had swords and helmets decorated with finely crafted gold. This ceremonial axe is made of iron. The patterns are of inlaid silver.

DWARFS

Dwarfs were small, clever, cunning and often greedy. They hoarded precious stones and metals underground, where they lived. They were despised by the gods who enslaved them and made them mine silver and work as smiths. But many were wise and skilled in magic and metalcraft. The dwarfs made weapons for the gods and jewellery for goddesses, whom they tried to woo.

▶ This illumination from an Icelandic manuscript shows a king cutting chains from a kneeling giant. Imagine the size of the giant if he stood up.

◀ In this illustration by Arthur Rackham from Wagner's Ring cycle of operas, the dwarf Mime (Regin) is hard at work trying to re-forge a broken sword for Siegfried (Sigurd).

Twilight of the Gods

THE VIKINGS thought the first world ended at a great battle called Ragnarok, which means the twilight of the gods. After the death of Balder there were many signs that the world was threatened.

Loki's punishment for Balder's death was to be tied over jagged rocks in a cave, where a snake dropped poison on to his face. His wife, Sigyn, caught the poison in a bowl, but when she left to empty it, the pain of the drops made Loki shudder in agony – and the earth shook. The land quaked, trees were uprooted, and a violent storm hurled ships on to the rocks.

Then Midgard froze over, and all humans died, except for one couple who hid in the branches of Yggdrasil. The sun and moon were devoured by the terrible wolves that chased them. The stars fell and the world was dark.

THE GREAT BATTLE
Loki and Fenrir broke free. The World Serpent surged up with the waves over the land, and Loki rode in on

VIOLENT WORLD
In the stories of the Norse gods, the world begins with heat and ice, and ends with flames and floods. Iceland is known even today as the land of ice and fire. It is in an area subject to earthquakes and

▼ Loki, bound to a rock, was tortured with snake poison. But, together with his monstrous son Fenrir, he had revenge on the gods, though he himself was slain by Heimdall.

▼ This 19th-century illustration shows the start of Ragnarok, which ended with a great fire and, according to Icelandic legends, was followed by the rebirth of a better world.

the crest of the wave in a ship filled with giants and other enemies of the gods.

Then, at Asgard, Heimdall sounded the last battle call. Odin led his warriors from Valhalla to slay his enemies. But Fenrir opened wide his jaws and killed Odin. Loki and Heimdall slaughtered each other. Thor slew Jormungand, but died from the serpent's poison. Tyr died fighting Garm. Odin's warriors battled with giants and monsters. In the end the fire giants set Asgard ablaze and all was destroyed.

A NEW WORLD

Following the battle, the sea rose as high as Yggdrasil and a new, fresh, green world arose from the ocean. A new sun lit the world. The couple who sheltered in Yggdrasil emerged to start a new race of humans, gods and animals who would live in peace and harmony.

volcanoes. When a volcano erupts on land there are flames and smoke. When one erupts underwater, it may cause an earthquake, and a huge destructive wave may roll over the land. Perhaps the story of Ragnarok is of a real, not a mythical, disaster.

▶ The Vikings were used to the horrors of battle. This illustration shows an attack on the English coast. The Saxons of England lived in dread of Viking raids, because the attackers were so ruthless and bloodthirsty.

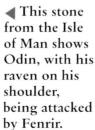

◀ This stone from the Isle of Man shows Odin, with his raven on his shoulder, being attacked by Fenrir.

GLOSSARY

Aesir Family of gods living in Asgard, the chief of whom was Odin.

altar Table-like stone on which animals and sometimes people were sacrificed; a place of offering in a temple, and later in a church.

archaeologists People who study the past by searching for buried evidence of human settlement, such as ruins, pottery, tombs and rubbish tips.

Asgard Home of the gods.

Balder Son of Odin and Frigg, the god of light who was killed by Loki's trickery.

bard Another name for a poet.

berserk Behaving in a frenzied manner like Viking warriors who became so crazed that they felt no pain.

boar Wild animal related to a pig.

ceremonial Formal action or object used in a ceremony or ritual.

chariot Kind of cart, usually two-wheeled, pulled by animals.

dwarfs Small supernatural beings, skilled in craftwork, but untrustworthy.

elves Supernatural beings, who could be either good (light elves) or bad (dark elves). See also nix; kobold.

falcon Bird of prey, trained for use in hunting.

fertile Able to grow crops or, in an animal or human, able to have young.

festival Holiday in honour of a god, when people feast, dance, make music and hold special ceremonies, including sacrifices.

fiord Deep inlet of the sea, a common feature of the Scandinavian west coast.

forge Furnace, or workshop containing a furnace; or to heat and shape metal.

Frey and Freya Twin children of the god Njord and the giantess Skadi.

Frigg Goddess wife of Odin.

funeral pyre Fire on which the bodies of the dead were burned.

Germanic Refers to people who settled mainly in northwest Europe, including Scandinavia, England, Germany etc. See map on page 31.

giants Supernatural beings, the enemies of the gods, who lived in a stronghold called Utgard.

gilt Layer of gold or substance that looks like gold laid over metal, wood or other material.

Hel Land of the dead, ruled by the ugly and unforgiving Hel.

horn Drinking vessel made from the hollowed horn of an animal.

illumination Miniature picture painted in a manuscript.

inlaid One substance, such as gold or other metal, set into another, usually in a pattern.

kobold Spirit thought to live in barns and stables that helped poor people by doing household tasks for them.

legend Story that may or may not be true, but usually based on an actual event, that becomes known by everyone.

Loki The trickster, lived in Asgard where he amused the gods but his mischief eventually turned to evil.

longship Viking warship, with one big sail and many oars.

mead Alcoholic drink made from honey and water.

Midgard The world of humans, linked by the rainbow bridge to Asgard.

mistletoe Plant once thought to be magical, or sacred, because it has no roots; it is a parasite.

myth Story, supposedly true, that explains how the world came to be as it is.

Nibelungs Another name for dwarfs in Richard Wagner's opera cycle *The Ring of the Nibelungs*.

nix A mischievous kind of water-spirit.

Norn One of three goddesses who spun the threads of fate; when one broke, a person died.

Norse Scandinavian.

Northlands Scandinavia and German-speaking lands further east.

Odin Father and king of all the gods, and the most wise.

pagan Person who believes in many gods and nature spirits.